Look at Us Glow!

By Cameron Macintosh

Contents

Things That Glow in the Sea

My home is way down
in the sea!

It is dim down here,
but I can glow.

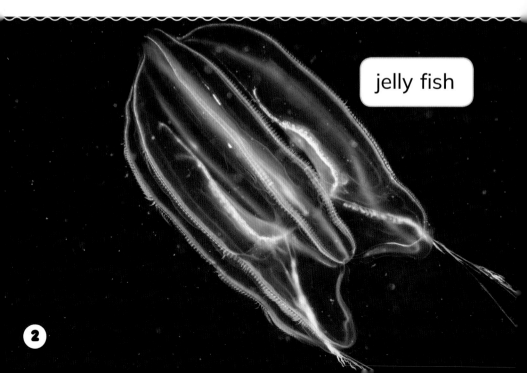

jelly fish

My glow helps me get away
from big fish that hope to eat me!

I'm a big fish that can glow, too.

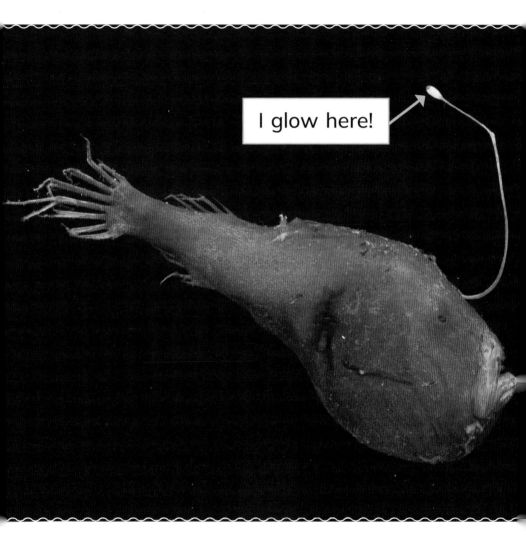

I glow here!

I show little fish my glow,
and they swim up to me.

If they are too slow,
I get them!

Yum!

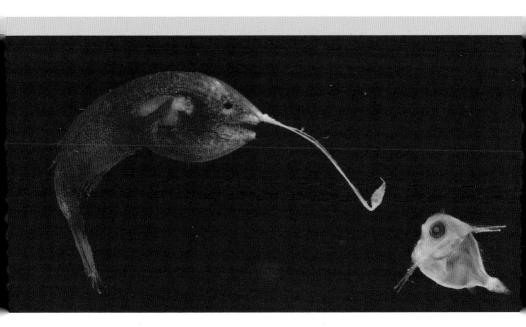

I'm a squid that can glow.

I am on my own a lot.

My glow helps me be safe.

Big fish see me, and they think
I look like the moon.

They will not eat me!

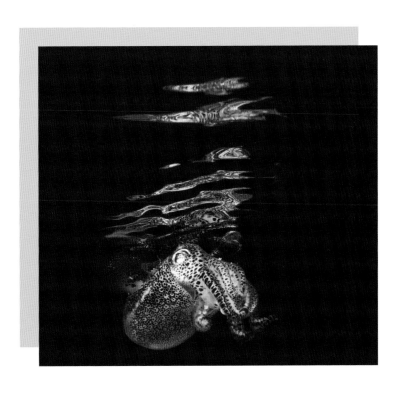

Bugs That Glow

I'm a bug that glows.

My glow can stop frogs
from snacking on me!

I find my bug friends
as they glow.

I can not miss them!

I'm a bug in an egg that glows.

I hang long, thin ropes
down to get little bugs to eat.

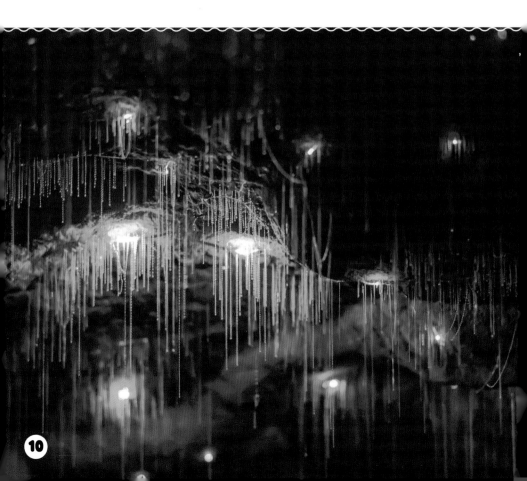

When I grow big,
the end of me glows!

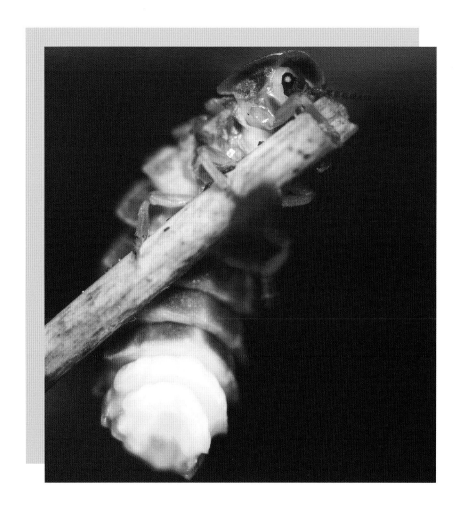

Plants That Glow

Some plants glow, too!

We glow to bring bugs to us.

The bugs help us grow.

It helps us a lot that
we can glow.

Look at us glow!

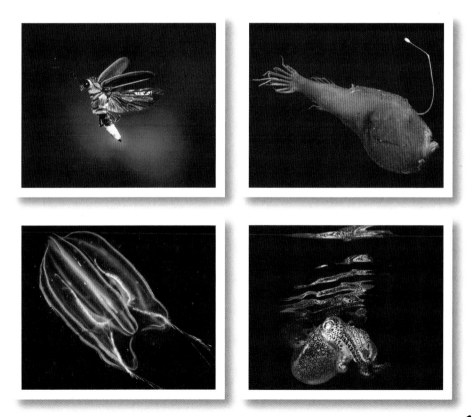

CHECKING FOR MEANING

1. Why does a jelly fish glow? *(Literal)*

2. Why does the big fish have a part that glows? *(Literal)*

3. How do bugs help plants to grow? *(Inferential)*

EXTENDING VOCABULARY

glow	Listen to the sound at the end of the word *glow*. How many other words can you make that have the long /o/ sound at the end? Are the letters making that sound always the same?
hope	What does it mean to *hope*? Do you know another word with a similar meaning? E.g. wish, dream. What is something you hope you will be able to do soon?
ropes	What are *ropes* in this text? What other words could be used that have a similar meaning? E.g. threads, strings, cords.

MOVING BEYOND THE TEXT

1. What is the main reason the living things in this text glow?

2. What are other ways living things can stay safe from things that might eat them?

3. What time of day do you think these living things glow best? Why?

4. What other things do you have that glow? How do you use them?

SPELLINGS FOR THE LONG /o/ VOWEL SOUND

o	oa	ow	o_e	oe

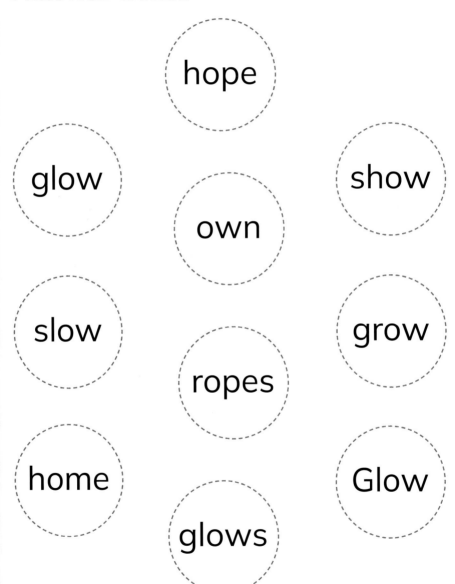

hope

glow

show

own

slow

grow

ropes

home

Glow

glows